Powerful
Prayers
OF PROMISE
PRAYING THE PROMISES OF GOD OVER YOUR LIFE

INTRODUCTION

You know when I look back on my life I wasn't raised as a child or young adult to believe much in God's mercy. I wasn't told that God has many great promises in His Word for me as a child of God. As a result, I lead a reckless lifestyle which ultimately lead to drug use and becoming a criminal. I was even a satanist for a period of my life. But God rescued me as He has with so many others. I struggle with bipolar and depression now because of the drug use doing LSD. If you would like to read about my life story and testimony read my book From Hell to Heaven, about how I was an Irish mobster and Satanist who came to know Christ.

This book is by no means full of the only promises God has given us but the ones which God has revealed to me through His Word to share with you. God never promised that we wouldn't have problems but He won't keep us there!

In this book I write prayers claiming the promises of God over you. I read a book called Quantum Faith by Ann Capps which talks about the power of the spoken word, the power of speaking God's truth over our lives and that it even has an effect in the physical realm. I believe this and have witnessed it in my own life. That is why the title of this book is Powerful Prayers of Promise: Praying The Promises of God Over Your Life. When we say something in Jesus' name it has power! There is power behind those words. I may repeat certain scriptures in this book to emphasize different promises. It also reinforces this promise in our minds. It's hard for us to stay in a negative mindset when we're saying positive things to ourselves from God's Word and claiming His promises over our lives. The scripture says the power of life and death is in the tongue. Our words give life when they are positive words! That is why we must fill our minds with God's Word and speak aloud His promises to us.

Promise 1:

Eternal Life!

John 3:16

"For God so loved the world, that He gave His only begotten Son, that whosoever believeth in Him should not perish, but have everlasting life.

Act 16:31

"And they said, Believe on the Lord Jesus Christ, and thou shalt be saved, and thy house."

John 10:28-30

"And I give unto them eternal life; and they shall never perish, neither shall any man pluck them out of my hand. My father, which gave them m, is greater than all' and no man is able to pluck them out of my Father's hand. I and my Father are one."

1 John 5:11

"And this is the record, that God hath given to us eternal life, and this life is in his Son."

1 John 5:13

"These things have I written unto you that believe on the name of the Son of God; that ye may know that ye have life eternal,and that ye may believe on the name of the Son of God."

Romans 6:23

"For the wages of sin is death; but the gift of God is eternal life through Jesus Christ our Lord."

John 17:3

"And this is life eternal, that they might know thee the only true God, and Jesus Christ, whom thou hast sent."

John 3:36

"He that believeth on the Son hath everlasting life; and he that believeth not the Son shall not see life; but the wrath fo God abideth on him."

1 Timothy 6:12

"Fight the good fight of faith, lay hold on eternal life, whereunto thou art also called, and hast professed a good profession before many witnesses."

John 4:14

"But whosoever drinketh of the water I give shall never thirst; but the water that I shall give him shall be in him a well of water springing up into everlasting life."

1 Timothy 1:16

"Howbeit for this cause I obtained mercy, that in me first Jesus Christ might shew forth all longsufferig, for a pattern to them which should hereafter believe on him to life everlasting.

Romans 5:21

"That as sin hath reigned unto death, even so might grace reign through righteousness unto eternal life by Jesus Christ our Lord."

Pray this prayer with me:

"Lord I thank you for your promise of salvation

and eternal life! I just claim this promise over my life and rebuke Satan and any lies about my eternal security in you Lord. Help me to seek to bring others to You so that they might have eternal life also. Thank You that I have a home in heaven. Help me to always remember Lord when I am going through trials in this life they are only temporary. My eternal destiny is with You. I just pray that others would see the light of Christ in me and be drawn towards You. In Jesus' Name, Amen."

Promise 2:

He is Your Protector, Helper and Will Keep You From Evil

2 Thessalonians 3:3

"But the Lord is faithful, who shall establish you, and keep *you* from evil."

2 Timothy 4:18

"And the Lord shall deliver me from every evil work, and will preserve [me] unto his heavenly kingdom: to whom [be] glory forever and ever. Amen."

Proverbs 19:23

"The fear of the LORD [tendeth] to life: and [he

that hath it] shall abide satisfied; he shall not be visited with evil."

Psalms 23:4

"Yea, though I walk through the valley of the shadow of death, I will fear no evil: for thou [art] with me; thy rod and thy staff they comfort me."

Isaiah 54:17

"No weapon that is formed against thee shall prosper; and every tongue [that] shall rise against thee in judgment thou shalt condemn. This [is] the heritage of the servants of the LORD, and their righteousness [is] of me, saith the LORD."

Deuteronomy 28:7

"The LORD shall cause thine enemies that rise up against thee to be smitten before thy face: they shall come out against thee one way, and flee before thee seven ways."

2 Samuel 22:3-4

"The God of my rock; in him will I trust:[he is] my shield, and the horn of my salvation, my high tower, and my refuge, my saviour; thou savest me from violence. I will call on the LORD, [who is]worthy to be praised: so shall I be saved from mine enemies."

James 4:7

"Submit yourselves therefore to God. Resist the devil, and he will flee from you."

Psalms 138:7

"Though I walk in the midst of trouble, thou wilt revive me: thou shalt stretch forth thine hand against the wrath of mine enemies, and thy right hand shall save me."

Psalms 121:7

"The LORD shall preserve thee from all evil: he shall preserve thy soul."

Hebrews 13:6

"So that we may boldly say, The Lord is my helper, and I will not fear what man shall do unto me."

Exodus 14:14

"The Lord shall fight for you, and ye shall hold your peace."

Psalms 118:6

"The Lord is on my side; I will not fear: what can man do to me?"

Psalms 119:114

"Thou art my hiding place and my shield: I hope in thy word."

Psalms 3:3

"But thou, O Lord, art a shield for me; my glory, and the lifter of mine head."

Romans 8:31

"What shall we then say to these things? If God be for us, who can be against us?"

Proverbs 30:5

"Every word of God is pure: he is a shield unto them that put their trust in him."

2 Samuel 22:32

"For who is God, save the Lord? And who is a rock, save our God?"

Psalm 34:22

The Lord redeemeth the soul of his servants: and none of them that trust in him shall be desolate."

Psalms 121:1-2

"(A Song of degrees.) I will lift up mine eyes unto the hills, from whence cometh my help. My help [cometh] from the LORD, which made heaven and earth."

Psalms 54:4

"Behold, God [is] mine helper: the Lord [is] with them that uphold my soul."

Pray this prayer with me:

"Thank you Lord for the promise that You are my Protector, my Helper and will keep me from evil. I just bind Satan over my life and all his dark forces in your Name Lord. I claim this promise over every area of my life Lord that You are my Protector, and Helper and that You will keep me from evil. Thank You Lord that Your Word says You fight for me. Help me when I am in trouble to look to You for help. Let me not rely on my own strength Lord, but Yours. Thank You Lord that Your Word says if You be for me who can be against me? Thank You for protecting me Lord from spiritual attacks of Satan and physical as well. Give me the confidence Lord to know that You are always with me, In Your Name I pray, Amen."

Promise 3:

Hope

Romans 15:13

"Now the God of hope fill you with all joy and peace in believing, that ye may abound in hope, through the power of the Holy Ghost."

Jeremiah 29:11 (NKJV)

"For I know the thoughts I think toward you, says the Lord, thoughts of peace and not of evil, to give you a future and hope."

Hebrews 11:1

"Now faith is the substance of things hoped for, the evidence of things not seen."

1 Corinthians 13:13

And now abideth faith, hope, charity, these three; but the greatest of these is cherity."

Romans 5:3-4

"And not only so, but we glory in tribulations also: knowing that tribulation worketh patience;And patience, experience; and experience, hope."

Psalms 31:24

"Be of good courage, and he shall strengthen your heart, all ye that hope in the Lord."

Romans 8:25

"But if we hope for that we see not, then do we with patience wait for it."

Micah 7:7

"Therefore will I look unto the Lord; I will wait for the God of my salvation: my God will hear me."

Psalms 130:5

"I wait for the Lord, my soul doth wait, and in his word I do hope."

Lamentations 3:24

"The Lord is my portion, saith my soul; therefore will I hope in him."

Psalms 33:22

"Let thy mercy, O Lord, be upon us, according as we hope in thee."

Romans 5:5

"And hope maketh not ashamed; because the love of God is shed abroad in our hearts by the Holy Ghost which is given unto us."

1 Peter 1:3

"Blessed be the God and Father of our Lord Jesus Christ, which according to his abundant mercy hath begotten us again unto a lively hope by the resurrection of Jesus Christ from the dead."

Ephesians 4:4

"There is one body, and one Spirit, even as ye are called in one hope of your calling."

Colossians 1:27

"To whom God would make known what is the riches of the glory of this mystery among the Gentiles; which is Christ in you, the hope of glory."

Pray this prayer with me:

"Thank you Lord for the hope I have in you! I just claim this promise of hope over every area of my life and rebuke Satan and any thoughts of hopelessness, depression, fear, worry, or anxiety. Thank You Lord that You have given me hope and a future. Thank You that I can have hope in Your mercy, oh Lord. Thank You for the hope of glory, eternal life and a home in heaven with You. Thank You Lord that Your Word says when I call to You, You will hear me. Help me to have hope through trials and tribulations Lord knowing they won't last forever. In Your mighty Name I pray, Amen!"

Promise 4:

God Has a Plan for Your Life and Will Guide You

Jeremiah 29:11 (NKJV)

"For I know the thoughts that I think toward you, says the Lord, thoughts of peace, and not of evil, to give you a future and a hope."

Proverbs 3:5-6

"Trust in the LORD with all thine heart; and lean not unto thine own understanding. In all thy ways acknowledge him, and he shall direct thy paths."

Romans 8:28

"And we know that all things work together for good to them that love God, to them who are the called according to [his] purpose."

Ecclesiastes 3:1

"To every [thing there is] a season, and a time to every purpose under heaven,"

Proverbs 16:9

"A man's heart deviseth his way: but the LORD directeth his steps."

Isaiah 58:11

"And the LORD shall guide thee continually, and satisfy thy soul in drought, and make fat thy bones: and thou shalt be like a watered garden, and like a spring of water, whose waters fail not."

Jeremiah 1:5

"Before I formed thee in the belly I knew thee; and before thou camest forth out of the womb I sanctified thee, [and] ordained thee a prophet unto the nations."

Romans 12:2

"And be not conformed to this world: but be ye transformed by the renewing of your mind, that ye may prove what [is] that good, and acceptable, and perfect, will of God."

Psalms 27:14

"Wait on the LORD: be of good courage, and he shall strengthen thine heart: wait, I say, on the LORD."

Psalms 32:8

"I will instruct thee and teach thee in the way in the way which thou shalt go: I will guide thee with mine eye."

1 Corinthians 2:9

"But as it is written, Eye hath not seen, nor ear heard, neither have entered into the heart of man, the things which God hath prepared for them that love him."

Psalms 37:23

"The steps of a [good] man are ordered by the LORD: and he delighteth in his way."

Pray this prayer with me:

"Thank you Lord that you have a plan for my life Lord, that you have a hope and a future for me and that you will direct my paths! I just claim this promise over my life Lord and pray that you guide me in every area of my life. Show me the specific plan You have for my life Lord. Thank You that Your Word says even though I make plans, You direct my steps. Give me divine direction in every area of m life Lord, in my work, my finances and in my relationships. Thank You Lord that Your Word says You will guide me in very way. I pray that you equip me with everything I need to pursue the plan You have for my life and that I would pursue it with boldness and courage. In Jesus' Name, Amen!"

Promise 5:

He Will Give His Angels Charge Over You

Psalms 91:11

"For he shall give his angels charge over thee, to keep thee in all thy ways."

Hebrews 1:14

"Are they not all ministering spirits, sent forth to minister for them who shall be heirs of salvation?

Psalms 34:7

"The angel of the LORD encampeth round about them that fear him, and delivereth them."

Matthew 24:31

"And he shall send his angels with the great sound

of a trumpet, and they shall gather together his elect from the four winds, from one end of heaven to the other."

Matthew 18:10

"Take heed that ye despise not one of these little ones; for I say unto you, That in heaven their angels do always behold the face of my Father which is in heaven."

Pray this prayer with me:

Lord, thank You for your promise of the protection of angels. Lord I just claim this promise over my life and Your divine protection through Your angels who will keep me in all my ways Lord. I just pray Lord that You surround my family and friends with Your angels. Help me to always be mindful Lord that as I go about my daily life You are protecting me. Help me to have peace of mind knowing that You send Your angels to protect me even when I am unaware of it. In Jesus' precious Name I pray, Amen!"

Promise 6:

God Loves You

John 3:16

"For God so loved the world, that he gave his only begotten Son, that whosoever believeth in him should not perish, but have everlasting life."

Romans 5:8

"But God commendeth his love toward us, in that, while we were yet sinners, Christ died for us."

1 John 4:19

"We love him, because he first loved us."

1 John 4:10

"Herein is love, not that we loved God, but that he loved us, and sent his Son [to be] the propitiation for our sins."

Romans 8:35

"Who shall separate us from the love of Christ? [shall] tribulation, or distress, or persecution, or nakedness, or peril, or sword?"

Romans 8:37

"Nay, in all things we are more than conquerors through him that loved us."

Romans 8:39

"Nor height, nor depth, nor any other creature, shall be able to separate us from the love of God, which is in Christ Jesus our Lord."

Jeremiah 31:3

"The LORD hath appeared of old unto me, [saying], Yea, I have loved thee with an everlasting love: therefore with lovingkindness have I drawn thee."

1 John 4:8

"He that loveth not knoweth not god; for God is love."

Galatians 2:20

"I am crucified with Christ: nevertheless I live; yet not I, but Christ liveth in me: and the life which I now live in the flesh I live by the faith of the Son of God, who loved me, and gave himself for me."

Zephaniah 3:17

"The LORD thy God in the midst of thee [is] mighty; he will save, he will rejoice over thee with joy; he will rest in his love, he will joy over thee with singing."

1 John 15:13

"Greater love hath no man than this, that a man lay down his life for his friends."

Ephesians 3:19

"And to know the love of Christ, which passeth knowledge, that ye might be filled with all the fullness of God."

1 Corinthians 13:13 (NKJV)

"But now abide faith, hope, love, these three; but the greatest of these is love."

Pray this prayer with me:

"Thank You for the promise of your love Lord! I just claim this promise over myself right now and pray that your love would fill my heart for others. Thank You Lord that You were willing to lay down Your life on the cross for me. Help me to show the same love You show to me to all those around me, my friends, family, neighbors and strangers. Help me to rest in Your love as the scripture says Lord. Help my words, actions and attitudes to reflect Your love Lord. In Jesus' Name I pray, Amen!"

Promise 7:

His Mercy

Lamentations 3:22-23

"It is of the Lord's mercies that we are not consumed, because his compassions fail not. They are new every morning: great is thy faithfulness."

Ephesians 2:4-5

"But God, who is rich in mercy, for his great love wherewith he loved us, Even when we were dead in sins, hath quickened us together with Christ, (by grace ye are saved)."

Joel 2:13

"And rend your heart, and not your garments, and turn unto the LORD your God: for he [is] gracious and merciful, slow to anger, and of great kindness, and repenteth him of evil."

1 John 1:9

"If we confess our sins, he is faithful and just to forgive us our sins, and to cleanse us from all unrighteousness."

Psalms 86:5

"For thou, Lord, [art] good, and ready to forgive; and plenteous in mercy unto all them that call upon thee."

Deuteronomy 4:31

"(For the LORD thy God [is] a merciful God;) he will not forsake thee, neither destroy thee, nor forget the covenant of thy fathers which he sware unto them."

Luke 6:36

"Be ye therefore merciful, as your father also is merciful."

1 Peter 1:3

"Blessed [be] the God and Father of our Lord Jesus Christ, which according to his abundant mercy hath begotten us again unto a lively hope by the resurrection of Jesus Christ from the dead."

Pray this prayer with me:

"Thank You for the promise of Your mercy Lord! Your mercies are new every morning. I just claim this promise of Your mercy over my life and thank You for it Lord. Help me not to live in self-condemnation Lord, but to realize You have separated my sins from me as far as the East is from the West. Help me to extend the same mercy towards others Lord that You extend towards me. I just rebuke Satan in the Name of the Lord Jesus Christ and any condemnation he would try to get me to bring upon myself. Thank You Lord that You are a God of mercy. In Jesus' Name I pray, Amen!"

Promise 8:

He Wants to Prosper You

3 John 2:2

"Beloved, I wish above all things that thou mayest prosper and be in health, even as my soul prospereth."

John 15:7

"If ye abide in me, and my words abide in you, ye shall ask what ye will, and it shall be done unto you."

Matthew 7:7-8

"Ask, and it shall be given you; seek, and ye shall find; knock, and it shall be opened unto you: for everyone that asketh receiveth; and he that seeketh findeth; and to him that knocketh it shall be opened."

Romans 8:28

"And we know all things work together for good to them that love God, to them who are the called according to [his] purpose."

Hebrews 11:6

"But without faith [it is] impossible to please [him]: for he that cometh to God must believe that he is, and [that] he is a rewarder of them that diligently seek him."

Psalms 91:16

"With long life will I satisfy him, and shew him my salvation."

John 10:10

"The thief cometh not, but for to steal, and to kill, and to destroy: I am come that they might have life, and that they might have [it] more abundantly."

Proverbs 22:4

"By humility [and] the fear of the LORD [are] riches, and honour, and life."

Psalms 1:3

"And he shall be like a tree planted by the rivers of water, that bringeth forth his fruit in his season; his leaf also shall not wither; and whatsoever he doeth shall prosper."

Pray this prayer with me:

"Thank You Lord that You want me to prosper! I just claim this promise over every area of my life including my finances, my job, my health, and my relationships that I would prosper! I just pray Your prosperity over other believers I know Lord in my family, my church, neighbors, friends and strangers who are believers in You. Help me Lord to be humble, as You say before humility and the fear of the Lord come riches, honor and life. In Jesus' Name, Amen!"

Promise 9:

Encouragement and Comfort

1 Thessalonians 5:11

"Wherefore comfort yourselves together, and edify one another, even as also ye do."

Isaiah 43:2

"When thou passest through the waters, I will be with thee; and through the rivers, they shall not overflow thee: when thou walkest through the the fire, thou shalt not be burned; neither shall the flame kindle upon thee."

Joshua 1:9

"Have I not commanded thee? Be strong and of a good courage; be not afraid, neither be thou dismayed: for the Lord thy God is with thee whithersoever thou goest."

Deuteronomy 31:8

"And the Lord, he it is that doth go before thee; he will be with thee, he will not fail thee, neither forsake thee: fear not, neither be dismayed."

2 Corinthians 1:3-4

"Blessed be God, even the Father of our Lord Jesus Christ, the Father of mercies, and the God of all comfort; Who comforteth us in all our tribulation, that we may be able to comfort them which are n any trouble, by the comfort wherewith we ourselves are comforted of God."

Psalms 121:1-2

"I will life up mine eyes unto the hills, from whence cometh my help. My help cometh from the Lord, which made heaven and earth."

Hebrews 10:24-25

"And let us consider one another to provoke unto love and to good works: Not forsaking the assembling of ourselves together, as the manner of some is; but exhorting one another: and so much the more, as ye see the day approaching."

Psalms 31:24

"Be of good courage, and he shall strengthen your heart, all ye that hope in the Lord."

Romans 8:31

"What shall we then say to these things? If God be for us, who can be against us?"

Romans 15:5

"Now the God of patience and consolation grant you to be likeminded one toward another according to Christ Jesus."

Romans 15:2

"Let every one of us please his neighbour for his good to edification."

Psalm 90:17

"And let the beauty of the Lord our God be upon us:and establish thou the work of our hands upon us; yea, the work of our hands establish thou it."

Luke 12:6-7

"Are not five sparrows sold for two farthings, and not one of them is forgotten before God? But even the very hairs of your head are all numbered. Fear not therefore: ye are of more value than many sparrows."

Proverbs 27:17

"Iron sharpeneth iron; so a man sharpeneth the countenance of his friend."

Pray this prayer with me:

"Lord thank You for this promise of comfort and encouragement from You as well as other believers. I just claim this promise over my life and rebuke Satan and any discouragement he may try to bring upon me. Thank You Lord that You are always there to comfort and encourage me through trials and tribulations. Thank You for giving me friends and fellow believers to comfort and encourage me as well. I pray that I would be a comforter and an encouragement to others. Help me to attend church regularly Lord so that I can be around other believers and we can encourage one another. In Jesus' Name I pray, Amen!"

He Will Be Your Refuge, Fortress and High Tower

Psalms 18:2

"The LORD is my rock, and my fortress, and my deliverer; my God, my strength, in whom I will trust; my buckler, and the horn of my salvation, and my high tower."

Psalms 31:3

"For thou [art] my rock and my fortress; therefore for thy name's sake lead me, and guide me."

Psalms 71:3

"Be thou my strong habitation, whereunto I may continually resort: thou hast given commandment to save me; for thou [art] my rock and my fortress."

Psalms 91:2

"I will say of the LORD, [He is] my refuge and my fortress: my God; in him will I trust."

Psalms 144:2

"My goodness, and my fortress; my high tower, and my deliverer; my shield, and [he] in whom I trust; who subdueth my people under me."

Jeremiah 16:19

"O LORD, my strength, and my fortress, and my refuge in the day of affliction, the Gentiles shall come unto thee from the ends of the earth, and shall say, Surely our fathers have inherited lies, vanity, and [things] wherein [there is] no profit."

Proverbs 18:10

"The name of the LORD is a strong tower: the righteous runneth into it, and is safe."

Pray this prayer with me:

"Lord thank You for the promise that You are my Refuge, Fortress, and High Tower, that I can run to You in times of trouble. I just claim this promise over my life right now Lord. Thank You Lord that

I can trust in You for protection. Keep me in all my ways Lord. I just pray Your protection over my family, friends, neighbors and other believers Lord. I pray that I would always turn to You first Lord in times of trouble. Thank You Lord that You are a safe haven I can go to. In Jesus' Name I pray, Amen!"

Promise 11:

Peace

Numbers 6:24-25

"The Lord bless thee, and keep thee: The Lord make his face shine upon thee, and be gracious unto thee: The Lord lift up his countenance upon thee, and give thee peace."

John 16:33

"These things have I spoken unto you, that in me ye might have peace. In the world ye shall have tribulation: but be of good cheer; I have overcome the world."

John 14:27

"Peace I leave with you, my peace I give unto you: not as the world giveth, give I unto you. Let not your heart be troubled, neither let it be afraid."

Philippians 4:6-7

"Be careful for nothing; but in every thing by prayer and supplication with thanksgiving let your requests be made known unto God. And the peace of God, which passeth all understanding, shall keep your hearts through Christ Jesus."

2 Thessalonians 3:16

"Now the Lord of peace himself give you peace always by all means. The Lord be with you all."

Psalm 4:8

"I will both lay me down in peace, and sleep: for thou, Lord, only makest me dwell in safety."

Isaiah 26:3

"Thou wilt keep him in perfect peace, whose mind is stayed on thee; because he trusteth in thee."

Colossians 3:15

"And let the peace of God rule in your hearts, to the which also ye are called in one body; and be ye thankful."

Jude 1:2

"Mercy unto you, and peace, and love, be multiplied."

James 3:18

"And the fruit of righteousness is sown in peace of them that make peace."

Psalms 119:65

"Great peace have they which love thy law: and nothing shall offend them."

Philippians 4:9

"Those things, which ye have both learned, and received, and heard, and seen in me, do: and the God of peace shall be with you."

Romans 8:6

"For to be carnally minded is death; but to be spiritually minded is life and peace."

Pray this prayer with me:

"Lord You are the one who calmed the storms, You are the God of peace. Lord I just claim Your peace over my life right now. You say in Your Word that the mind that is stayed on You is at perfect peace. Keep me from worry, anxiety, and depression in my life Lord. I declare myself free from these things in the Name of the Lord Jesus Christ! I claim that I will have peace always as it is in 2 Thessalonians 3:16. Thank You for the peace which surpasses all understanding Lord, in your Name, Amen!"

Promise 12:

Courage

Deuteronomy 31:6

"Be strong and of a good courage, fear not, nor be afraid of them: for the LORD thy God, he [it is] that doth go with thee; he will not fail thee, nor forsake thee."

Deuteronomy 31:7

"And Moses called unto Joshua, and said unto him in the sight of all Israel, Be strong and of a good courage: for thou must go with this people unto the land which the LORD hath sworn unto their fathers to give them; and thou shalt cause them to inherit it."

Deuteronomy 31:8

"And the Lord, he it is that doth go before thee; he

will be with thee, he will not fail thee, neither forsake thee: fear not, neither be dismayed.”

Joshua 1:9

“Have not I commanded thee? Be strong and of a good courage; be not afraid, neither be thou dismayed: for the Lord thy God is with thee whithersoever thou goest.”

1 Corinthians 16:13

“Watch ye, stand fast in the faith, quit you like men, be strong.”

2 Timothy 1:7

“For God hath not given us the spirit of fear; but of power, and of love, and of a sound mind.”

Psalms 23:4

“Yea, though I walk through the valley of the shadow of death, I will fear no evil: for thou art with me; thy rod and thy staff they comfort me.”

Psalms 31:24

“Be of good courage, and he shall strengthen your heart, all ye that hope in the Lord.”

John 14:27

"Peace I leave with you, my peace I give unto you: not as the world giveth, give I unto you. Let not your heart be troubled, neither let it be afraid."

Psalms 27:14

"Wait on the Lord: be of good courage, and he shall strengthen thine heart: wait, I say, on the Lord."

Mark 6:49-50

"But when they saw him walking upon the sea, they supposed it had been a spirit, and cried out: For they all saw him, and were troubled. And immediately he talked with them, and saith unto them, Be of good cheer: it is I; be not afraid."

Pray this prayer with me:

"Lord, You tell us constantly in these verses to be of good courage, and not to be afraid, just as Moses told Joshua and as You told the disciples when they saw You on the water. Lord thank You for the courage your Word says You have given me, not a spirit of fear, but of power, love, and a sound mind. I just claim this courage, Your courage, over myself right now and bind the enemy Satan and the spirit of fear in Your Name. I declare your courage over my life Lord, the courage your Word says you have given me. I pray that You give me boldness and courage as I witness to others Lord in sharing the gospel, in Jesus' Name, Amen!"

Promise 13:

Rest and Sleep

Psalms 127:2

"[It is] vain for you to rise up early, to sit up late, to eat the bread of sorrows: [for] so he giveth his beloved sleep."

Proverbs 3:24

"When thou liest down, thou shalt not be afraid: yea, thou shalt lie down, and thy sleep shall be sweet."

Matthew 11:28-29

"Come unto me, all [ye] that labour and are heavy laden, and I will give you rest. Take my yoke upon you, and learn of me; for I am meek and lowly in heart: and ye shall find rest unto your souls."

Psalms 4:8

"I will both lay me down in peace, and sleep: for thou, LORD, only makest me dwell in safety."

Psalms 23:2

"He maketh me to lie down in green pastures: he leadeth me beside the still waters."

Ecclesiastes 5:12

"The sleep of a labouring man [is] sweet, whether he eat little or much: but the abundance of the rich will not suffer him to sleep."

Psalms 37:7

"Rest in the Lord, and wait patiently for him: fret not thyself because of him who prospereth in his way, because of the man who bringeth wicked devices to pass."

Pray this prayer with me:

"Lord thank You for your promise of rest and sleep. I pray Lord that you will quiet the busyness of my day and that I will rest in you and get sleep. I just claim this promise of rest and sleep over my life right now. Lord thank You that Your Word says You make me to lie down in green pastures. Please help me Lord to take the time to get sleep. Thank You Lord that You say that I can lie down and sleep because You make me dwell in safety. Thank You Lord for Your protction while I sleep. Please calm any anxiey or wories from my day that I migt have. In Jesus' Name I pray, Amen!"

Promise 14:

Joy

Psalms 16:11

"Thou wilt shew me the path of life: in thy presence is fulness of joy.; at thy right hand there are pleasures for evermore."

1 Peter 1:8-9

"Whom having not seen, ye love; in whom, though now ye see him not, yet believing, ye rejoice with joy unspeakable and full of glory: Receiving the end of your faith, even the salvation of your souls."

John 16:24

"Hitherto have ye asked nothing in my name: ask, and ye shall receive, that your joy may be full."

Galatians 5:22-23

"But the fruit of the Spirit is love, joy, peace, longsuffering, gentleness, goodness, faith, meekness, temperance: against such there is no law."

Proverbs 23:24

"The father of the righteous shall greatly rejoice: and he that begetteth a wise child shall have joy of him."

1 Timothy 6:17

"Charge them that are rich in this world, that they be not high minded, nor trust in uncertain riches, but in the living God, who giveth us richly all things to enjoy."

Pray thiis prayer with me:

"Lord You say in Your Word that You give us richly all things to enjoy, and the in Your presence is fullness of joy. Give me Your joy I pray Lord in my everyday life. I just claim Your promise of joy now over my life and bind Satan and all negative thoughts, including worry, depression, and anxiety in Jesus' Name! Thank you for Your joy Lord. Thank You for the joy I have in Your salvation and that I am Your child. When I go through trials and tribulations, help me to always be mindful of the joy You have given me. Amen.”

Promise 15:

Forgiveness

Ephesians 4:32

"And be ye kind one to another, tenderhearted, forgiving one another, even as God for Christ's sake hath forgiven you."

Matthew 6:14

"For if ye forgive men their trespasses, your heavenly Father will also forgive you."

Colossians 3:13

"Forbearing one another, and forgiving one another, if any man have a quarrel against any: even as Christ forgave you, so also do ye."

2 Chronicles 7:14

"If my people, which are called by my name, shall

humble themselves, and pray, and seek my face, and turn from their wicked ways; then will I hear from heaven, and will forgive their sin, and will heal their land."

Luke 6:37

"Judge not, and ye shall not be judged: condemn not,and ye shall not be condemned: forgive, and ye shall be forgiven."

Proverbs 28:13

"He that covereth his sins shall not prosper: but whoso confesseth and forsaketh them shall have mercy."

Psalms 85:5

"For thou, Lord, art good, and ready to forgive; and plenteous in mercy unto all them that call upon thee."

Micah 7:18

"Who is a God like unto thee, that pardoneth iniquity, and passeth by the transgression of the remnant of his heritage? he retaineth not his anger for ever, because he delighteth in mercy."

Psalms 32:5

"I acknowledge my sin unto thee, and mine iniquity have I not hid. I said, I will confess my transgressions unto the Lord; and thou forgavest the iniquity of my sin. Selah."

Ephesians 1:7

"In whom we have redemption through his blood, the forgiveness of sins, according to the riches of his grace."

James 5:14-15

"Is any sick among you? let him call for the elders of the church; and let them pray over him, anointing him with oil in the name of the Lord: And the prayer of faith shall save the sick, and the Lord shall raise him up; and if he have committed sins, they shall be forgiven him."

Pray this prayer with me:

"Lord I just thank You for Your promise of forgiveness, the forgiveness of sin. I just claim this promise over my life right now and rebuke Satan and any thoughts of condemnation which he may bring against me. Lord You say that if I forgive others their trespasses, You will frgive me of mine. Please help me to be patient with others around me

Lord. Help me to have a forgiving heart towrds them. Help me not to judge others Lord. Thank You Lord that You have separated my sin from me as far as the East is from the West. Help me to always turn to You Lord whenI sin and imediately ask Your forgiveness. Help me to be patient and forgiving towards my family, friends, neighbors and strangers Lord. In Jesus' Name I pray, Amen!"

Promise 16:

Faith

Romans 12:13

"For I say, through the grace given unto me, to every man that is among you, not to think of himself more highly than he ought to think; but to think soberly, according as God hath dealt to every man the measure of faith."

James 2:17

"Even so faith, if it hath no works, is dead, being alone."

Romans 1:17

"For therein is the righteousness of God revealed from faith to faith: as it is written, the just shall live by faith."

2 Corinthians 5:7

"For we wank by faith, not by sight."

Hebrews 11:1

"Now faith is the substance of things hoped for, the evidence of things not seen."

Ephesians 3:12

"In whom we have boldness and access with confidence by the faith of him."

Hebrews 11:6

"But without faith it is impossible to please him: for he that cometh to God must believe that he is, and that he is a rewarder of them that diligently seek him."

James 1:3

"Knowing this, that the trying of your faith worketh patience."

1 John 5:4

"For whatsoever is born of God overcometh the world: and this is the victory that overcometh the world, even our faith."

Mark 10:52

"And Jesus said unto him, Go thy way; thy faith hat made thee whole. And immediately he received his sight, and followed Jesus in the way."

Galatians 3:26-27

"For ye are all the children of God by faith in Christ Jesus. For as many of you as have been baptized into Christ have put on Christ."

Matthew 17:20

"And Jesus said unto them, Because of your unbelief: for verily I say unto you, if ye have faith as a grain of mustard seed, ye shall say unto this mountain, Remove hence to yonder place; and it shall remove; and nothing shall be impossible for you.."

Pray this prayer with me::

"Thank You Lord for giving me a measure of faith as it says in Your word, and that if I only have the faith of a mustard seed I can move mountains! Thank You for giving me more than a mustard seed of faith Lord, and thank You Lord that our faith overcomes the world as it says in your word Lord. I claim your promise of faith over every area of my life Lord, and I bind Satan the enemy and any thoughts of doubt he would try to bring into my mind. Lord help me to have faith and believe You for Your promises. Help me not to doubt Lord. Thank You that we walk by faith and not by sight. In Jesus' Name, Amen!"

Promise 17:

He Hears Our Prayers

1 John 5:14-15

"And this is the confidence that we have in him, that, if we ask any thing according to his will, he heareth us: And if we know that he hear us, whatsoever we ask, we know that we have the petitions that we desired of him."

John 15:7

"If ye abide in me, and my words abide in you, ye shall ask what ye will, and it shall be done unto you."

Isaiah 65:24

"And it shall come to pass, that before they call, I will answer; and while they are yet speaking, I wll hear."

John 15:16

"Ye have not chosen me, but I have chosen you, and ordained you, that ye should go and bring forth fruit, and [that] your fruit should remain: that whatsoever ye shall ask of the Father in my name,he may give it you."

Psalms 37:4-5

"Delight thyself also in the LORD; and he shall give thee the desires of thine heart. Commit thy way unto the LORD; trust also in him; and he shall bring [it] to pass."

Micah 7:7

"Therefore I will look unto the LORD; I will wait for the God of my salvation: my God will hear me."

Pray this prayer with me:

"Thank You Lord for the promise that You hear my prayers! I just claim this promise over my life right now by the Name of Jesus Christ. Lord thank You that You say in Your Word that I can ask anything according to Your will and I will receive it! Help me to remember to pray for others Lord. Help my day not to be so busy that I do not take the time to spend time I prayer with You. Thank You Lord that

You say if I delight myself in You, You will give me the desires of my heart. Thank You Lord that I can come to You with all of my fears, concerns, worries and anxities Lord. Help me to always be ready to turn to You in prayer when I am in need or trouble Lord. Help me to be a prayer warrior Lord! Help me to fight the battle against Satan and spiritual darkness on my knees Lord. In Your Name I pray, Amen!"

Ask Anything According to God's Will and You Will Receive it

1 John 5:14

"And this is the confidence that we have in him, that, if we ask any thing according to his will, he heareth us."

Mark 11:24

"Therefore I say unto you, What things soever ye desire, when ye pray, believe that ye receive [them], and ye shall have [them]."

Matthew 7:7-8

"Ask, and it shall be given you; seek, and ye shall find: knock, and it shall be opened unto you: For every one that asketh receiveth; and he that seeketh findeth; and to him that knocketh it shall be opened."

John 14:13-14

"And whatsoever ye shall ask in my name, that will I do, that the Father may be glorified in the Son. If ye shall ask anything in my name, will do [it]."

John 15:7

"If ye abide in me, and my words abide in you, ye shall ask what ye will, and it shall be done unto you."

Matthew 21:22

"And all things, whatsoever ye shall ask in prayer, believing, ye shall receive."

Luke 11:13

"If ye then, being evil, know how to give good gifts unto your children: how much more shall [your] heavenly Father give the Holy Spirit to them that ask him."

John 16:24

"Hitherto have ye asked nothing in my name: ask, and ye shall receive, that your joy may be full."

Pray this prayer with me:

Thank You Lord that Your Word says if I ask anything according to Your will, I will receive it! I just claim this promise over every area of my life Lord. Help me to seek the tings You want for my life Lord, not my will, but Your's be done. Thank You that You want to give me good things as Your child. Help me not to be selfish in my prayers but to pray for the needs of others as well. Thank You that Your Word says You will supply all of my needs Lord acording to Your riches and glory in Christ Jesus. Bless me, my friends, family, neighbors and other believers Lord with good things! In Your precious Name I pray, Amen!"

Promise 19:

Blessings

Jeremiah 17:7-8

"Blessed is the man that trusteth in the LORD, and whose hope the LORD is. For he shall be as a tree planted by the waters, and that spreadeth out her roots by the river, and shall not see when heat cometh,
but her leaf shall be green; and shall not be careful in the year of drought, neither shall cease from yielding fruit."

Numbers 6:24-26

"The LORD bless thee, and keep thee: The LORD make his face shine upon thee, and be gracious unto thee: The LORD lift up his countenance upon thee, and give thee peace."

Exodus 23:25

"And ye shall serve the LORD your God, and he shall bless thy bread, and thy water; and I will take sickness away from the midst of thee."

Deuteronomy 30:16

"In that I command thee this day to love the LORD thy God, to walk in his ways, and to keep his commandments and his statutes and his judgments, that thou mayest live and multiply: and the LORD thy God shall bless thee in the land whither thou goest to possess it."

Psalm 34:8

"O taste and see that the LORD is good: blessed is the man that trusteth in him."

Matthew 5:6

"Blessed are they which do hunger and thirst after righteousness: for they shall be filled."

Malachi 3:10

"Bring ye all the tithes into the storehouse, that there may be meat in mine house, and prove me now herewith, saith the LORD of hosts, if I will not open you the windows of heaven, and pour you out a blessing, that there shall not be room enough to receive it."

Matthew 5:9

"Blessed are the peacemakers: for they shall be called the children of God."

 Psalm 119:2

"Blessed are they that keep his testimonies, and that seek him with the whole heart."

Proverbs 10:22

"The blessing of the Lord, it maketh rich, and he addeth no sorrow with it."

Pray this prayer with me:

"Lord Your Word says the blessing of the Lord it maketh rich! Lord I just claim this promise of blessings over every area of my life. Lord, You say blesed are the peacemakers. Help me to be a peacemaker Lord. Thank You Lord for everything You have blessed me wit in my life. Thank You for my friends, family, my church, my pastor, my home and providing for all my neeeds. I just pray a blessing over all of my friends, family and neighbrs Lord as well as other believers I Christ. May You bles thm richly and abundantly Lord in every way. Help me to always remember how and what and who You hve blessed me with Lord. I bnd Satan in Your Name Lord and the stealing of ay joy in my life that he would try to bring upn me by trying to make me believe that You are not a good Father. Thank You for blessing me with the gift of salvation Lord in Christ. In the precious Name of Jesus I pray, Amen!"

Promise 20:

Friendship

John 15:14-15

"Ye are my friends, if ye do whatsoever I command you. Henceforth I call you not servants; for the servant knoweth not what his lord doeth: but I have called you friends; for all things that I have heard of my Father I have made known unto you."

Proverbs 18:24

"A man that hath friends must shew himself friendly: and there is a friend that sticketh closer than a brother."

John 15:13

"Greater love hath no man than this, that a man lay down his life for his friends."

Pray this prayer with me:

"Thank You Lord that you are my friend! I just claim Your promise of friendship over my life right now in Your Name. Thank You for the friendship of others Lord, especially fellow believers. Help me to be a person who makes friends easily Lord. Help me to be a good friend to those around me. Thank You that I ave a friend to look to in You Lord when I am in need of fellowship. Thank You Lord that I never have to be lonely because You are always by my side. Thank You for Your wonderful git of salvation Lord, and that You were willing to lay down Your life for me, Your friend. Please help me to be a person who reaches out to those in need of friendship Lord. I pray this in Jesus' precious Name, Amen!"

Promise 21:

Give and You Will Receive

Luke 6:38

"Give, and it shall be given unto you; good measure, pressed down, and shaken together, and running over, shall men give into your bosom. For with the same measure that ye mete withal it shall be measured to you again."

Pray this prayer with me:

"Lord I thank You for Your promise that if I give I will receive. I Just pray that You help me to give with a cheerful heart. I claim this promise over every area of my life of giving and receiving. Help me to give with pure motives Lord, not so that I can get from others but so that I can be a blessing to those around me. I pray for various missions organizations Lord and Christian organizations doing Your work Lord that they would be blessed financially and in every other way Lord for the work they are ding for You. I pray that You give me a heart for giving to these mission groups Lord and giving to the poor and those in need. I know that You will reward me for this in Your own way Lord. Thank You for supplying all my needs Lord so I can give to others. Help me to have a heart of gratitude for what You have given me and will give to me Lord. In Jesus' Name I pray, Amen!"

Promise 22:

He Will Provide for All Your Needs

Philippians 4:19

"But my God shall supply all your need according to his riches in glory by Christ Jesus."

Matthew 6:31-32

"Therefore take no thought, saying, What shall we eat? or, What shall we drink? or, Wherewithal shall we be clothed? (For after all these things do the gentiles seek:) for your heavenly Father knoweth that ye have need of all of these things."

Matthew 7:11

"If ye then, being evil, know how to give good gifts unto your children, how much more shall your Father which is in heaven give good things to them that ask him?"

Luke 12:24

"Consider the ravens: for they neither sow nor reap; which neither have storehouses nor barn; and God feedeth them: how much more are ye better than the fowls?"

Psalms 34:10

"The young lions do lack, and suffer hunger: but they that seek the LORD shall not want any good [thing]."

Philippians 4:6 (NKJV)

"Be anxious for nothing, but in everything by prayer and supplication, with thanksgiving, let your requests be made known to God."

Pray this prayer with me:

"Dear Lord, I thank You for Your promise that You will supply all my needs. I just claim this promise over every area of my life, that You will supply all my needs. Lord, help me not to feel anxious or worried about my finances, relationships, my job or any other area of my life. Help me to look to You Lord as my Provider and the One who supplies all my needs. Thank You Lord that Your

Word says You feed even the ravens and I am more valuable than them. Help those I know who are in need Lord that You would bless them and supply everything they need including, money, relationships, housing, food and all of their essential needs Lord. Help me to be someone who gives to those in need Lord. I pray this in Jesus' Name,   Amen!"

Promise 23:

Eternal Riches

Matthew 6:19-20

"Lay not up for yourselves treasures on earth, where moth and dust doth corrupt, and where thieves break through and steal: But lay up for yourselves treasures in heaven, where neither moth nor dust doth corrupt, and where thieves do not break through nor steal."

Luke 12:33

"Sell that ye have, and give alms; provide yourselves bags which wax not old, a treasure in the heavens that faileth not, where no thief approacheth, neither moth corrupteth."

1 Timothy 6:17-19

"Charge them that are rich in this world, that they be not highminded, nor trust in uncertain riches, but in the living God, who giveth us richly all things to enjoy; That they do good, that they be rich in good works, ready to distribute, willing to communicate; Laying up in store for themselves a good foundation against the time to come, that they may lay hold on eternal life."

Revelation 22:12

"And, behold, I come quickly; and me reward [is] with me, to give every man according as his work shall be."

Luke 14:13-14

"But when thou makest a feast, call the poor, the maimed, the lame, the blind: And thou shalt be blessed; for they cannot recompense thee: for thou shalt be recompensed at the resurrection of the just."

Matthew 6:3-4

"But when thou doest alms, let not thy left hand know what thy right hand doeth: That thine alms may be in secret: and thy Father which seeth in secret himself shall reward thee openly."

Matthew 19:21

"Jesus said unto him, If thou wilt be perfect, go

[and] sell that thou hast, and give to the poor, and thou shalt have treasure in heaven: and come [and] follow me."

John 14:2

"In my Father's house are many mansions: if it were not so, I would have told you. I go to prepare a place for you."

Pray this prayer with me:

"Lord thank You for Your promise of eternal riches and that I have a mansion in heaven! I just claim this promise over my life right now. Help me Lord to lay up treasures in heaven as Your Word says. Thank You for the greatest eternal treasure of all which is eternal life. Help me to be heavenly minded and not earthly minded Lord. Help me to be a giving person, not so that I will get in return, but knowing that You will reward me in heaven for doing so. Thank You for preparing a place for me Lord. Help me to realize that though I may not be rich by the world's standards, I am rich by heavenly standards and by Your standards Lord. Thank You for being such a good heavenly Father Lord and a rewarder of those who do good. In Jesus' Name I pray, Amen!"

Promise 24:

Christ Will Return for You

Matthew 24:36

"But of that day and hour knoweth no [man], no, not the angels of heaven, but my Father only."

1 Corinthians 15:52

"In a moment, in the twinkling of an eye, at the last trump: for the trumpet shall sound, and the dead shall be raised incorruptible, and we shall be changed."

Matthew 25:13

Watch therefore, for ye know neither the day nor the hour wherein the Son of man cometh."

Matthew 24:27

"For as the lightning cometh out of the east, and

shineth even unto the west; so shall also be the coming of the Son of man."

Hebrews 9:28

"So Christ was once offered to bear the sins of many; and unto them that look for him shall he appear the second time without sin unto salvation."

Matthew 24:44

"Therefore be ye also ready: for in such an hour that ye think not the Son of man cometh."

Luke 21:27-28

"And then they shall see the Son of man coming in a cloud with great power and great glory. And when these things begin to come to pass, then look up, and lift up your heads; for your redemption draweth nigh."

1 Thessalonians 5:1-2

"But of the times and the seasons, brethren, ye have no need that I write unto you. For yourselves know perfectly that the day of the Lord so cometh as a thief in the night."

Pray this prayer with me:

"Lord thank You for the promise of Your return! I Just claim this promise over my life and the hope that it gives me. Thank You that though I may experience troubles in this life, I have the hope of Your return. Come back quickly Lord! I look forward to my eternal home with You in great expectancy! Thank You for saving me Lord. As the world around me crumbles I look to the heavens for Your soon return. I pray that others I know who are not saved would come to salvation in You so that they can be prepared for Your return as well. As the scripture says You are coming as a thief in the night. Help me to live a holy life and be ready for Your Second Coming! Thank You Lord that You say behold I come quickly! In Your precious Name I pray, Amen!"

Promise 25:

He Will Never Leave You or Forsake You!

Deuteronomy 31:8

"And the LORD, he [it is] that doth go before thee; he will be with thee, he will not fail thee, neither forsake thee: fear not, neither be dismayed."

Hebrews 13:5

"[Let your] conversation [be] without covetousness; [and be] content with such things as ye have: for he hath said, I will never leave thee, nor forsake thee."

Matthew 28:20

Teaching them to observe all things whatsoever I have commanded you: and, lo, I am with you alway, [even] unto the end of the world. Amen."

1 Chronicles 28:20

"And David said to Solomon his son, Be strong and of good courage, and do [it]: fear not, nor be dismayed: for the LORD God, [even] my God, [will be] with thee; he will not fail thee, nor forsake thee, until thou hast finished all the work for the service of the house of the LORD."

Pray this prayer with me:

"Lord thank You for the promise that You will never leave me nor forsake me no matter what I do. I just claim this promise over my life right now and bind Satan and any lies he would try to give me in regards to this promise. Help me to realize Lord that You are always there for me when I need You. I pray that I will look to You in my time of need. Thank You Lord that You will never abandon me. Thank You Lord that even though I sin, You are still with me. Help me to remember that You are with me always all the way into eternity in heaven. Help me to be there for others Lord like You are there for me. Thank You for Your faithfulness. In Jesus' Name I pray, Amen!"

Promise 26:

He is Your Healer

Psalm 147:3

"He healeth the broken in heart, and bindeth up their wounds."

James 5:14-15

"Is any sick among you? let him call for the elders of the church; and let them pray over him, anointing him with oil in the name of the Lord: and the prayer of faith shall save the sick, and the Lord shall raise him up; and if he have committed any sins, they shall be forgiven him."

James 5:16

"Confess your faults one to another, and pray one for another, that ye may be healed. The effectual fervent prayer of a righteous man availeth much."

Isaiah 53:5

"But he was wounded for our transgressions, he was bruised for our iniquities: the chastisement of our peace was upon him; and with his stripes we are healed."

2 Kings 20:5

"Turn again, and tell Hezekiah the captain of my people, Thus saith the LORD, the God of David thy father, I have heard thy prayer, I have seen thy tears: behold, I will heal thee: on the third day thou shalt go up unto the house of the LORD."

Exodus 15:26

"If thou wilt diligently hearken to the voice of the LORD thy God, and wilt do that which is right in his sight, and wilt give ear to his commandments, and keep all his statutes, I will put none of these diseases upon thee, which I have brought upon the Egyptians: for I am the LORD that healeth thee."

Luke 4:18

"The Spirit of the Lord is upon me, because he hath anointed me to preach the gospel to the poor; he hath sent me to heal the brokenhearted, to preach deliverance to the captives, and recovering of sight to the blind, to set at liberty them that are bruised."

Psalm 107:20

"He sent his word, and healed them, and delivered them from their destructions."

Pray this prayer with me:

"Lord thank you for the promise that You are my Healer! I claim this promise over every area of my life including my physical body and my emotions. I pray Lord that you heal those who are sick that I know and pray that you heal me from any physical sickness and all negative thoughts including fear, doubt, worry, depression and anxiety. I rebuke you Satan in the Name of the Lord Jesus and command you to take your hands off of my physical body as well as my emotions. Thank You Lord that You say 'I am the God that healeth thee.' Please help me to always remember to turn to You Lord when I am sick and in need of physical or emotional healing. Amen!"

Promise 27:

He is Your Confidence

John1 5:14

"And this is the confidence we have in him, that, if we ask any thing according to his will, he heareth us."

Proverbs 28:1

"The wicked flee when no man pursueth: but the righteous are bold as a lion."

Proverbs 3:26

"For the LORD shall be thy confidence, and shall keep thy foot from being taken."

Pray this prayer with me:

"Lord thank You for the promise that You are my confidence. I pray Lord that You make me bold as a lion, that You give me the confidence and boldness of a lion. I just claim this promise over my life Lord that You are my confidence and I just pray against any spirit of timidity or fear in me that it would leave in Jesus' Name. Give me boldness in my witness for You Lord. Help me not to fear what others think of me Lord. Give me a healthy confidence in myself and in You. Help me to have confidence in all my relationships Lord. Thank You Lord that I can come with confidence before Your throne, and that if I ask anything according to Your will You will hear me. Amen!"

Promise 28:

Ultimately You Will Overcome Pain, Suffering and Tribulation

Revelation 21:4

"And God shall wipe away all tears from their eyes; and there shall be no more death, neither sorrow, nor crying, neither shall there be any more pain: for the former things are passed away."

Romans 12:12

"Rejoicing in hope; patient in tribulation; continuing instant in prayer."

John 16:33

"These things I have spoken unto you, that in me ye might have peace. In the world ye shall have tribulation: but be of good cheer; I have overcome the world."

Romans 5:3

"And not only [so], but we glory in tribulations also: knowing that tribulation worketh patience."

Romans 8:18

"For I reckon that the sufferings of this present time [are] not worthy [to be compared] with the glory that shall be revealed in us."

2 Corinthians 12:9

"And he said unto me, My grace is sufficient for thee: for my strength is made perfect in weakness. Most gladly therefore will I rather glory in my infirmities, that the power of Christ may rest upon me."

Pray this prayer with me:

"Thank You Lord for your promise that ultimately I will overcome pain, suffering, and tribulation in life eternal with You. I pray that You will help me to overcome these trials through Your joy in this life, rejoicing in hope. Please help me to be patient through trials and tribulations. I just claim this promise over my life now and rebuke Satan and all his lies about my times of trials and tribulation. Help me as the scripture says Lord to stay in prayer through times of trial. I just pray Lord that I will see trials and tribulations in this life as an opportunity to glorify You Lord and to draw closer to You. I know Your grace is sufficient to get me through anything Lord. Help me keep my eyes on You and my eternal home. In Jesus' Name, Amen!"

Promise 29:

Wisdom

Proverbs 2:6

"For the LORD giveth wisdom: out of his mouth cometh knowledge and understanding."

James 1:5

"If any of you lack wisdom, let him ask of God, that giveth to all men liberally, and upbraideth not; and it shall be given him."

James 3:7

But the wisdom that is from above is first pure, then peaceable, gentle, and easy to be entreated, full of mercy and good fruits, without partiality, and without hypocrisy."

Matthew 7:24

"Therefore whosoever heareth these sayings of mine, and doeth them, I will liken him unto a wise man, which built his house upon a rock."

Proverbs 11:2
\
"When pride cometh, then cometh shame: but with the lowly is wisdom."

Proverbs 15:33

"The fear of the LORD is the instruction of wisdom; and before honour is humility."

Daniel 2:23

I thank thee, and praise thee, O thou God of my fathers, who hast given me wisdom and might, and hast made known unto me now what we desired of thee: for thou hast made known unto us the king's matter.

Pray this prayer with me:

"Lord I just thank You for the promise of wisdom! I just claim this promise over every area of my life including my finances, my relationships, and my decisions. Help me to be humble Lord as the scripture says so I can be a wise person. Thank

You that You say You give wisdom liberally Lord to all who ask! Help me to seek wise counsel Lord from others such as my pastor and friends who are believers in Christ. Help me not to make rash or foolish decisions Lord in my finances or other areas of my life. Help me to look to You Lord and Your Word as the ultimate source of wisdom. Help me to have the wisdom of Solomon Lord. Guide me in all my thoughts and decisions. Give me understanding Lord. Help me to speak words of wisdom to others Lord. In Jesus' Name I pray, Amen!"

Promise 30:

Power

2 Timothy 1:7

"For God hath not given us the spirit of fear; but of power, and of love, and of a sound mind."

Acts 1:8

"But ye shall receive power, after that the Holy Ghost is come upon you: and ye shall be witnesses unto me both in Jerusalem, and in all Judaea, and in Samaria, and to the uttermost part of the earth."

Luke 10:19

"Behold, I give you power to tread on serpents and scorpions, and over all the power of the enemy: and nothing shall by any means hurt you."

2 Corinthians 12:9

"And he said unto me, My grace is sufficient for thee: for my strength is made perfect in weakness. Most gladly therefore will I rather glory in my infirmities, that the power of Christ may rest upon me."

Ephesians 3:20

"Now unto him that is able to do exceeding abundantly above all that we ask or think, according to the power that worketh in us."

Luke 24:49

"And, behold, I send the promise of my Father upon you: but tarry ye in the city of Jerusalem, until ye be endued with power from on high."

Isaiah 40:29

"He giveth power to the faint; and to [them that have] no might he increaseth strength."

Pray this prayer with me:

"Lord thank You for the promise of power to be a witness for You and power over the enemy, Satan, and a spirit of power. I just claim this over every area of my life Lord Your promise of power for

Your glory. Help me not to seek power for my own personal gain but to further Your work and for the benefit of others Lord. Help me not to have a spirit of fear or timidity but Your Spirit Lord. Help me to realize that any power I have comes from You Lord. I pray that I walk in humility and not in pride Lord, that You give me the power to stand up for what is right! Help me to not be a timid Christian Lord, but a believer who walks in a spirit of power over Satan! Help me to exercise the spirit of power over the enemy and in my witness for You. In Jesus' Name, Amen!"

Promise 31:

Endurance and Strength

Isaiah 41:10

"Fear thou not; I [am] with thee: be not dismayed; for I [am] thy God: I will strengthen thee; yea, I will help thee; yea, I will uphold thee with the right hand of my righteousness."

Isaiah 40:31

"But they that wait upon the LORD shall renew [their] strength; they shall mount up with wings as eagles; they shall run, and not be weary; [and] they shall walk, and not faint."

Psalms 31:24

"Be of good courage, and he shall strengthen your heart, all ye that hope in the Lord."

Exodus 15:2

"The Lord [is] my strength and my song, and he is become my salvation: he [is] my God, and I will prepare him an habitation; my father's God, and I will exalt him."

Pray this prayer with me:

"Lord I just pray that You give me Your strength. Thank You for the promise of Your strength and endurance. I just claim this promise of strength and endurance and that You are my strength Lord as Your Word says over my life right now. Help me not to be weary Lord in doing Your work and my daily tasks. Help me to keep my eyes on You Lord. I pray that I would not over-commit myself dear Lord, but that You help me to find a balance in my daily routines and commitments to You and others. Help me to enjoy my work Lord and have a love for life and others. I pray this in Jesus' Name, Amen!"

Promise 32:

He Will Help You Overcome Temptation

1 Corinthians 10:13

"There hath no temptation taken you but such as is common to man: but God [is] faithful, who will not suffer you to be tempted above that ye are able; but will with the temptation also make a way to escape, that ye may be able to bear [it]."

James 5:7

"Submit yourselves therefore to God. Resist the devil, and he will flee from you."

Ephesians 6:11

"Put on the whole armour of God, that ye may be able to stand against the wiles of the devil."

1 John 5:4

"For whatsoever is born of God overcometh the world: and this is the victory that overcometh the world, [even] our faith."

Pray this prayer with me:

"Thank You Lord that You will help me overcome temptation and will provide a way of escape. I just claim this promise over my life right now and bind Satan and command him and all temptation to sin to flee in Your Name Lord Jesus. Help me Lord when I am tempted to sin to look toward You. Lead me not into temptation but deliver me from evil as it says in the Lord's Prayer. Thank You Lord that You are a merciful and forgiving heavenly Father, so that I know when I do sin I can come to You for mercy and forgiveness. Thank You Lord that You say in Your Word You will provide a way of escape from temptation. Help me to have the desire to live a life that is pleasing to You. In Your precious Name I pray, Amen!"

Promise 33:

He is Your Deliverer

2 Samuel 22:2

"And he said, The LORD is my rock, and my fortress, and my deliverer."

Psalms 18:2

"The LORD is my rock, and my fortress, and my deliverer; my God, my strength, in whom I will trust; my buckler, and the horn of my salvation, and my high tower."

Psalms 40:17

"But I am poor and needy; yet the Lord thinketh upon me: thou art my help and my deliverer; make no tarrying, O my God."

Psalms 144:2

"My goodness, and my fortress; my high tower, and my deliverer; my shield, and he in whom I trust; who subdueth my people under me."

Psalms 34:19

"Many are the afflictions of the righteous: but the LORD delivereth him out of them all."

Pray this prayer with me:

"Thank You lord for the promise that You are my deliverer, and that my afflictions may be many but You will deliver me out of them all! I just claim this promise over my life right now and Your deliverance Lord in every area of my life. Thank You Lord that when I am going through trials, tribulations and temptation I can look to for deliverance. Help me to always look to You first to deliver me from my troubles and not to seek my own answers to my problems. I just rebuke Satan in Your Name Lord Jesus, and pray that You deliver me and anyone else I know who may be under demonic oppression. Deliver me Lord from fear, anxiety, worry, depression and doubt. Thank You Lord that You are always by my side. Thank You for delivering me from the power of sin and death through the cross Lord. In Jesus' Name I pray, Amen!"

Promise 34:

The Lord's Goodness

Nahum 1:7

"The LORD is good, a strong hold in the day of trouble; and he knoweth them that trust in him.

Psalms 27:13

"I had fainted, unless I had believed to see the goodness of the LORD in the land of the living."

Exodus 18:19

"And Jethro rejoiced for all the goodness which the LORD had done to Israel, whom he had delivered out of the hands of the Egyptians."

Exodus 34:6

"And the LORD passed before him, and proclaimed, The LORD, the LORD God, merciful and gracious, longsuffering, and abundant in goodness and truth."

Psalms 31:19

"[Oh] how great [is] thy goodness, which thou hast laid up for them that fear thee: [which] thou hast wrought for them that trust in thee before the sons of men!"

Psalms 33:5

"He loveth righteousness and judgment: the earth is full of the goodness of the LORD."

Psalms 107:9

"For he satisfieth the longing soul, and filleth the hungry soul with goodness."

Pray this prayer with me:

"Thank You Lord for the promise of Your goodness! I just claim the promise of Your goodness over every area of my life. Help me to always remember Your goodness Lord even when I am going through difficult times in my life. Thank You Lord that You say You satisfy the longing soul and fill the ungry with goodness. Help me to share the goodness You have blessed me with to those around me. Help me to be grateful Lord for all the good things You have given me. Help me to think with a positive outlook on life Lord remembering all You have blessed me with. Thank You Lord that Your Word says You are abundant in goodness and truth. Help me to constantly remember these truths in my life Lord as I live day to day to serve You. In Jesus' Name I pray, Amen!"

Promise 35:

You Can Put Your Trust in Him

Jeremiah 17:7

"Blessed is the man who trusteth in the LORD,
and whose hope the LORD is."

Proverbs 3:5-6

"Trust in the LORD with all thine heart; and lean
not unto thine own understanding. In all thy ways
acknowledge him, and he shall direct thy paths."

Psalms 56:3

"What time I am afraid, I will trust in thee."

Psalms 143:8

"Cause me to hear thy lovingkindness in the
morning; for in thee do I trust: cause me to know
the way wherein I should walk; for I lift up my

soul unto thee."

Psalms 37:3

"Trust in the LORD, and do good; so shalt thou dwell in the land, and verily thou shalt be fed."

Pray this prayer with me:

"Thank You Lord that I can put my trust in You for everything, when I have needs, when I am afraid, everything Lord. I just claim this promise that I can put my trust in You over every area of my life. I just bind Satan and all the attacks of the enemy in Jesus' Name and any lies Satan would try to feed me that would cause me not to trust in You Lord. Thank You Lord that when I trust You with my whole heart, lean not unto my own understanding and in all my ways acknowledge You, You will direct my path. Help me not to trust in m own strength, knowledge or wisdom Lord but to trust You in everything and for everything in my life. Thank You Lord that I can trust You for blessings and to give me good things. Thank You Lord that I can put my trust in Your promise of salvation and eternal life through Your Son, Jesus Christ. Help me to trust You with my family Lord, my wealth, my possessions, my job, my relationships, my health and every other area of my life Lord. In Jesus' precious Name, Amen!"